#justacrumb

A Morsel of Inspiration from God's Word
for your Everyday Life

BILLY T. STATON, JR.

#justacrumb

DEDICATION

I want to dedicate this book to all of those who have dreams and you've stopped dreaming. Keep Dreaming and Keep Moving Forward! I also would like to dedicate this book to Jason Minor(nephew), Janice Perry(Cousin), Robert Garrison, Claudia Brown and The Providence St. John Baptist Church Family (PSJBC)

Well, I'm so excited to share with you another #justa-crumb devotional that will give you Encouragement, Motivation, and Inspiration to carry you through your day, week, and month. I was so overwhelmed by the many stories and testimonies from the 40-day devotional, that in my very own life it has done what the focus of this second devotional is: To Encourage, Motivate, and Inspire. So, I pray this #justacrumb devotional will speak loud and bring you closer to God, and make you stronger for yourself and everyone connected to you.......
May these stories and challenges give Encouragement, Motivation, and Inspiration so let's begin a new journey with the #justacrumb devotional.

CONTENTS

Day 1

God Will Provide
Philippians 4:19

I'm not a roller coaster ride, my wife and her sisters and brother like them, but I don't. There was one time we went to an amusement park, and my wife decided to ride the Grizzly at the Kings Dominion amusement park. So, I walked up to the ride with her but had not planned to ride. She got on and sat three or four seats from the front because she wanted to experience everything.

I was just standing there asking her, "Are you going to ride this by yourself?" And she said, "Yeah!" Out of nowhere, this guy got on next to her, and I told him, "No, man, that's mine." I was thinking that I didn't want him hugging my wife, or my wife hugging him. If she needed to hug or hold onto anyone, it was going to be me. So, I got on the ride thinking, "What in the world am I doing on this roller coaster?" As I'm on the roller coaster, I'm holding on tight; and she's telling me that I need to open my eyes so that I can see everything. The roller coaster is going up and down, this way and that way; and I'm doing it all for love because I love her and didn't want her hugging on some dude.

In this situation, God showed me that sometimes life takes you through some serious turns. Sometimes it takes you through some serious drops and twirls, and you may ask yourself, "What in the world am I doing?" Sometimes we have those questions and say, "God, I didn't know that putting my faith in you would bring so many problems, so many ups, and downs, and so many turns and twists." But, if you just hold on, He's got you. Don't let go! He's working something out of you and He's working something in you.

Have you ever had those situations where you ask God to do something RIGHT NOW, and He doesn't answer you? Do you find yourself asking, "Okay, God? What's going on? What are you doing?" It's like God is telling you to hold on. He's saying, "I haven't spoken, yet. And I haven't made a move, yet." Did you hear that? It's like God is saying, "Chill out. Relax. Breathe. I haven't spoken, yet. And I haven't made a move, yet. I WILL provide." God is telling us to relax, calm down, chill out, and breathe. He is telling us that He hasn't yet spoken or made a move, but He WILL provide. That gives me so much encouragement.

Philippians 4:19: "And this same God who takes care of me will supply all your needs from his glorious riches, which have been given to us in Christ Jesus." God will supply all our needs. Just stay the course. Continue to pray. Continue to believe in God. Continue to trust God. Don't lose strength, but look for Him to encourage you. No matter what it looks like, or what you're going through, or what the challenge is, GOD Will Provide

#justacrumb

Day 2

Sharing Is Caring
Philippians 2:3-4

God has blessed my wife and me with a beautiful home. It has been a place of fun, laughter, excitement, and the whole nine. Our home has been a place of refuge, strength, and encouragement for others. Any man knows that in your home, the basement belongs to you. That's where the man cave goes. Well, we have this wonderful home and I didn't get the basement for my man cave as I wanted.

I had plans for my man cave and had mapped out where my television, chairs, and everything would be. As I was writing and mapping out what I wanted, the salon where my wife was working shut down, and she asked me if she could bring her business home and use the space that I was planning to use. So being the great supportive husband I yielded my plans to make her happy, and we made it a full-service salon. All her clients came in and cried because they came in to see a full-fledged salon, which has been a blessing.

Recently, the basement suffered some damage, and God has blessed us so that we are now able to erect a wall down there. So, there's this wall that goes up, and my wife and I were talking about what we want to do in the basement; and she said that I could put up the wall and have my space – my man cave. I wanted the whole basement, but I couldn't get that because it belongs to me and my wife, my son, my sister, and my niece.

To all married couples (and even singles or those who want to remarry). You have to understand that nothing belongs to you when you get married, you are one. As a good friend of ours, Helen Holmes says, "1 + 1 = 1."

Sharing is vital to a marriage. You must share; I think a lot of marriages today are challenged because no one is sharing. If everything is all on one side of the coin, it's not sharing it's a dictatorship. If someone has the "you have what you have; keep what you have; don't mess with what

I have" attitude, that's not sharing. You're supposed to be one. Remember $1 + 1 = 1$. We must understand that in the covenant of marriage we need to share. We must look at each other and ask what we can do to be a blessing to the other.

This wall that I told you about is the wall of sharing. It's a display for the ladies and men that come into our house to see sharing. I want to encourage all of those who are married, who are looking to get married, and who want to remarry to share. The things in your life do not belong just to you.

If you say, "my money is my money," that's not sharing. When you get married, everything goes into one big pot. You can't say "my car is my car." You can't have an individual account, money under the mattress, and money at your aunt's house in case of emergency. That's deceit, that's hiding that's not sharing. Some marriages are suffering because there is no sharing. There is no sharing about how you feel or what we can do to be better. If there's no sharing, we can't grow.

I'm grateful that my wife and I are moving together. She had the idea to put the wall up to make my man cave possible. I think I'm going to put a code on my door; you may even have to have a special knock!

What would happen if more married couples would share? What would happen if more couples would look at how we could benefit by communicating and talking to each other about what moves we're going to make, instead of making a move and then coming back to explain the move? That's not sharing.

*Philippians 2:3-4, which talks about having the attitude of Christ: "Don't be selfish; don't try to impress others. Be humble, thinking of others as better than yourselves. Don't look out only for your own interests, but take an interest in others, too." The Bible tells us to have the attitude of Christ. The scriptures talk about women being submissive to your husband's as you are unto God. Husbands ought to love their wives as Christ loves the church. Do you see what's happening? In both accounts, submitting, serving, and sharing must be equal. There is no asking, "Why do I have to serve?"

Husband, you must serve your wife too. You must love her as Christ loves the church. You must be prepared to give yourself, to lay it all on the line for your wife. Wife, you must be submissive to your husband as you are to God. Philippians says that we should not be selfish. In other words, we should be sharing. We should not be thinking about what we want all the time, we should be looking not just at our own interests, but take an interest in others too. We shouldn't be looking at our own agendas, but at how "our" agenda can be addressed, reinforced, or encouraged. Don't be selfish, sharing is caring. Can you say that along with me? Sharing is caring.

The Lord will make a way when you start sharing; some of you are struggling right now in your marriage. Ask yourself if you're sharing, and if you are sharing, ask God to help you be better at sharing and pray that your spouse's heart will be turned towards God. Prayer works! There are countless testimonies of marriages that were on shaky ground (some were on no ground), but through prayer and fasting, God turned that thing around!

I'm praying for every married couple, that you start sharing. Some of the issues you're going through could be because you didn't share in listening or in conversation. It can't be what you want all the time. If it is, it's not sharing.

#justacrumb

Day 3

Seasons
1 Chronicles 12:32

In the spring of 2018, it was a cold start in the DC, MD, and VA areas and everybody was wondering why the season wasn't shifting. We had cold and rain, and I think it even snowed, and everyone was like "Oh my gosh! This is not supposed to be happening right now! It's supposed to be sunny outside. We're supposed to be enjoying ourselves." I was feeling like I should have been playing golf and enjoying defeating my golf buddies. But, everyone was feeling upset because the season had not changed.

A lot of us get sidetracked when the season doesn't change according to our timetable. We get frustrated. Everyone was frustrated because the season hadn't changed according to their expectations. The weathermen were telling us what should have been happening in the season, but the weatherman is not God. God is in control of the seasons.

Some of us have been going through major seasons – seasons of lack, seasons of depression, and seasons of health challenges. While going through these seasons, we are asking the Lord, "When is my tough season coming to a close?" Sometimes, we look at other people's situations and challenges and talk to them about what they encountered. They tell us things like, "My issue lasted this long, or here are the symptoms that I experienced," and we're listening for something that would tell us when our season might be ending. But we must remember to wait for what God says.

Keep in mind that seasons come and go, but what you do in your season is critical. You can't get upset when the season doesn't change on your timetable. God must work something out before the change happens. When we understand this, we understand that God is in control and knows exactly what He's doing and that He's in control of everything.

We have to understand the seasons and the time – observe what God is doing; relax and be calm; let God do what He is going to do. I know sometimes we want the change, the increase, the promotion, the marital situation, the home situation, and the financial situation to change NOW, but God is saying that He is in control.

1 Chronicles 12:32, which states, "From the tribe of Issachar, there were 200 leaders of the tribe with their relatives. All these men understood the signs of the times and knew the best course for Israel to take." These people understood the signs of the time.

The seasons are signs and times. When you understand the signs and times, you are observing when God is speaking and moving. When God is speaking and moving, you don't have to be impatient, frustrated, upset, or out of sorts because you need God to move now. You don't have to wonder when your change is coming, it's a season.

Sometimes God is working things out of you to get you prepared for what He is about to bring you to. We must study the signs so that we know what time it is. A lot of us are using our own timetables to determine where we should be, and we get confused and even sick because we don't know how to read the signs of the time. We need to take a lesson from the tribe of Issachar. They understood the signs of the time, you need to observe what God is doing, study the signs. This is why your prayer and scripture time is so critical. Prayer and study of the Bible will allow you to hear what God is telling you to do.

For some of you, it is not yet the time to launch the business, you must be patient. God knows exactly what He is doing. All we need to do is let Him do what He's doing. Be patient. Be anxious for nothing and let God work this thing out. Be attentive to the seasons and the times and understand what God is doing, so that when the season comes, you're ready.

There were 200 leaders and their relatives in the tribe of Issachar. They all understood the signs of the time and knew the best course to take. If you look at the background of this tribe, they studied the stars and the moon and nature and how things are moving. That's God! If you study nature and the wind and the sun and the rain, that's God. If you are observant, you will know when things are about to change. You can feel it. You can see God working. That will help you become more patient. It will help you know when your change is coming.

Some of your tough seasons are coming to an end. Things are getting better. You're coming through, just stay in prayer and the Word. God will tell you, and show you when your season is coming to an end. There are times when God will speak to you – through prayer and scripture, through strong and healthy associations with people whom you hold in high esteem and respect, who will be honest with you and will tell you that God is always speaking. So make sure you pay attention and move, speak, or stand still in your season until God gives instructions that will bring peace, strength, growth, and understanding.

The problem is that we don't always pay attention to the signs. We must obey and study the signs and times. It's all about seasons. Hold on! You are about to come out of your season. God is about to turn it around. Go back into prayer and back into the scripture and ask God to speak to you.

#justacrumb

Day 4

Follow Instructions
James 1:22

O ne of the things that I love about my wife is that she is excellent at cooking using recipes. She is a queen of recipes! She has a recipe for lasagna, one for ribs, one for pot pie, and so many more. In addition to that, I have done some thinking about what a recipe is. A recipe is a set of instructions that, if followed, yield the desired result. In our lives, we must follow instructions so that we get the results that the instructions tell us we will get.

My sister, Carla, is known for her potato salad and it is awesome! I recall one time we were at a family function and I asked her, "Why don't you add this ingredient to your potato salad?" She said, "That isn't in the recipe!" The next time we had a big function, I asked her if she would try something else, and her response was, "I'm not trying that, it's not in the recipe." You see, she watched her aunt make this recipe, and it is always amazing. So, Carla does it the same way she learned it. She will not deviate from the recipe, nor will she improvise because keeping with the recipe ensures that she gets the same amazing result every time.

Even I have a knack with my seafood salad (and nobody's allowed in the kitchen when I'm making my seafood salad. NOBODY!) My sister reminded me that nobody ever tells me how to make my seafood salad. I have a formula that I use to make it, and I'm not changing it because every time I do it, it is a great success!

Many of us are stuck in our thinking and our lives because we don't follow instructions. We are trying to create or improvise on a tried and true recipe. We try to bring our things into the mix because we are comfortable with what we've been doing. We don't want to do what the instructions say, but instead, want to do our own thing. We don't want to follow healthy instructions that will improve us.

I want to encourage you to simply follow instructions in the word of God – do what the instructions say you are to do. We so often won't make a move to follow instructions that will improve us, or better us, or strengthen us because we have been comfortable doing it our way. Even if we know what we are doing has had us stuck for a long time, we won't change.

James 1:22, which reads, "But don't just listen to God's word. You must do what it says. Otherwise, you are only fooling yourselves."

God is saying that we can't just hear his word, but we must put it into action. What has God's word told you to do that you have not done? You must follow God's instructions. Many of us are hitting a wall and are having no fulfillment because we are not following God's recipe. Many of us want to implement what we want and not what God is telling us to do.

As a pastor, most of my job is encouraging people to follow instructions. I only give to the people what God gives me. God gives it to me first, to apply it to my life, so that I can see how he can move in my life, too. What is so hard about following God's word?

Most of you reading this book are believers, the ones who have confessed Jesus as Lord, the ones who are submitted to the Lord. We need not just be hearers of his word, but doers, as well. If you read through the scriptures, you will notice that it's always the ones that God has the relationship with that he is trying to convince to follow instructions because the word works best when you apply it. Many folks hear the word and act on it to impress the pastor or to impress family and friends, but the pastor nor your family have any heaven or hell to put us in.

When was the last time you followed instructions? We often go through tremendous struggle, because we don't just do what God is saying. God tells us to love one another; forgive those who have mistreated us; obey those in authority; give honor where honor is due; and so much more. God has given us the ultimate map, the ultimate blueprint for living, and yet we still do what we want.

Some of you are on the brink of a breakthrough and change in your life, and all you need to do is follow instructions. Just follow instructions. Just do what God has told you to do.

I tried to get my sister to change her potato salad recipe, and I don't even make potato salad. She has a recipe that has been proven over time. It has never failed. It has been consistent over time. What would happen if we would be consistent with following God's instructions? You won't miss, you won't fail. You will be blessed coming in and blessed going out. What did God tell you to do? Just follow instructions.

I am so excited about being a self-published author.

Just a Crumb didn't come out years ago because I didn't follow instructions. I did not do what God told me to do, so God had to wake me in the middle of the night to ask me what he had told me to do. I had to repent and then went and did as he had instructed me.

Now, for you… What did God's word say? Don't give your opinion. What did God's word say to you? Whatever God tells you to do, whatever he tells you to say, I pray that he etches a scripture in your heart. If nothing else, remember James 1:22; and do what the word of God says.

Some of you have businesses, new endeavors, and things that God has been speaking to you. You know God is speaking to you when you have peace when you are being urged to take a faith leap. You must stop trying to do what you want to do. Follow what God's word says. Do what he told you to do.

#justacrumb

$$Day \ 5$$

Give Thanks
1 Thessalonians 5:16-18

O ver 20 years ago, I joined the First Baptist Church of Glenarden in Maryland where my father in ministry is Pastor John K. Jenkins, Sr. Being at First Baptist has molded, shaped, empowered, and equipped me. I have learned so many marvelous things there. There have been good and bad days there. One thing that I was blessed to be a part of was praise and worship.

I grew up as a young lad in a Pentecostal church, so I didn't see anything like praise and worship with its powerful songs and different flavor. Praise and worship spoke something different to me. It helped me better understand my relationship with the King of Kings and Lord of Lords. It helped me better understand who I am; and God helped to give me a way of living through praise and worship.

When I met my beautiful bride, she was listening to a station called WGTS 91.9 Christian Music Radio for Washington, D.C. and there were praise and worship on that station that I had never heard. And the music began to speak to me. Have you ever been in a situation where things have been so overwhelming, and you needed a song that would help encourage, inspire, and uplift you? There is a song by Don Moen entitled Give Thanks that would always speak to me:

Give thanks with a grateful heart.

Give thanks to the holy one.

Give thanks because he's given Jesus Christ his son.

And now let the weak say I am strong.

Let the poor say I am rich because of what the Lord has done for us.

Give thanks.

That song spoke to me, and now I want to encourage you to give thanks in everything.

Give thanks because of what the Lord has done. God has

done so much, and sometimes we can be so overwhelmed with pressures and the hustle and bustle that we forget to give thanks. Even in situations where you have no control, no matter the dilemma, the challenge, the problem, the situation, or the circumstance, you should give thanks. God is saying that we should give thanks with a grateful heart because he has given Christ his son.

I just want to encourage you to give God thanks, despite what you're going through. Stop listening to everyone's opinion. The Lord wants you to just talk with him. Some of us go through so many cycles, pains, and ups and downs. You feel no one understands or hears you. You must turn all your attention to him and let him speak to you.

1 Thessalonians 5:16-18, "Always be joyful. Never stop praying. Be thankful in all circumstances, for this is God's will for you who belong to Christ Jesus."

One day I asked God why there was always something. It was like there was something around every corner. I asked God what I should do at this time. He told me to take my mind off my problems and issues and just give him thanks.

That is what I encourage you to do, now. God will give you joy, peace, and a word. When you're thinking about your situation, you are trying to figure it out, but he just wants us to give it to him and give thanks.

You must start giving God thanks. Give him thanks! Thank him for waking you up. Thank him for allowing problems to come so that he can show his strength and his might and his power. Some of you are too down and too hard on yourselves, no matter what just remember to Give God Thanks.

#justacrumb

#justacrumb

Day 6

Put God First
Haggai 1:1-10

In this day and time, a lot of people do not put God first on their agenda. God is a second or third option. When it comes to serving God, there is no push. It is not seen as a necessity, especially for those who know about God. Sometimes we try to reject or neglect what we know and form our own opinions, though we know the truth.

Some people in the household of faith are going through unnecessary pressure, challenges, issues, and drama because God is not first. Everything else is first – your career, your job, your car, your house, your vacation, your fraternity, your sorority, your hairdo, your pedicure, and your manicure. God is fourth or fifth, not top on the list. He's way down there. We need to make God first.

When God is first, you won't do the things you've been doing, and you won't move without first consulting him. When God is first, you are listening to hear his voice before you hear someone else's. You're not seeking answers on social media, but you're going into your prayer closet and quiet time to hear what God is saying. When God is first, you don't listen to the opinions of others, but you are listening for God to speak to you. When God is first, you will do what God has told you to do.

Haggai 1:5-10 the scripture reads "look at what's happening around you." There is nothing that is functioning properly. Every time you try to make money, you lose it. Every time you eat, you're still hungry. Every time you drink water to quench your thirst, you're still thirsty. You wear clothing, but you're still cold. In other words, your basic needs are not met because God is not first.

My brother, Pastor Tyrone Stevenson, of Hope City Church, stated, "What's first is the only thing you don't let go of when trouble comes." If God is first, you don't let go of him when trouble comes. When God is first, you don't leave a church when trouble comes. When you leave a church because of trouble, it's like a kid coming to the playground with a ball and taking his ball, and going home because no one wants to play or have fun with him. But, what is interesting is that, often, the challenges that have come are the ones we have created.

When you put God first, you have a purpose. We see in Haggai that the people had a purpose.

They were supposed to go and build the house of God. However, they got off task and started investing in paneled houses. They took what was supposed to be used for the house of God, and started investing in themselves. Then, they decided that they would build the house of God when they thought the time was right. So, the man of God had to come and talk to them.

The man of God told them that they hadn't put God first. The people didn't realize they had to put God first for the purpose, but they also hadn't realized that putting God first was for their protection. The Bible says that their money was gone, they had no food, their clothing was not keeping them warm, and they were drinking water and was still thirsty. God says that when he's not first, it affects your necessities. When he's not first, your basic needs go lacking. When he's not first, you put money in your pocket and the pocket has holes in it. You work hard to get the money, but when you get it, you lose it. When God is first, it is for your protection. Your money won't be funny and your change won't be strange.

Some of you are eating, but you're not full. You're drinking water, but you're still thirsty. You have clothing, but you're still not warm, and; your basic needs are lacking because God is not first. Some of you have experienced not putting God first and it resulted in things not being right, things being broken down, things not working, or the loss of a job. God is saying that if you put him first, you will have a purpose, but provision will also be made. All I am saying is that you put God first, no matter where you are in life. If he's not first, put him first today. I put God first. I ask him, "God, what do you want me to say? God, what do you want me to do? God, where do you want me to go? God, should I invest in this business? God, you tell me what I need to do."

Put God first and watch him blow your mind. In my own life, I was supposed to write a devotional book, and I did not do it for five years. God was speaking through other people, but I kept rejecting it. I didn't listen and, finally, he had to wake me up one morning and say, "What did I tell you to do?"

My situation is so similar to what he is telling the people in Haggai 1. He says, "Look at what's happening around you," and then he goes on to say, "This is what you need to do." He says, "This is where you need to go to do what you need to do." He gives them instruction and then tells them where to find the wood to build the temple. When I did what God told me to do, God put into place everything I needed, and God blessed me so much (and he is still blessing me right now) because I did what he told me to do. He let the dew fall on my life all because I did what he told me to do.

God sent the dew when I did what he told me to do, and I am here to encourage you! The dew of favor, the dew of strength, the dew of confidence will fall in your life. We are so often looking for money, but sometimes we have to ask God to send the dew of encouragement, the dew of peace, the dew of direction, the dew of vision, the dew of purpose, and the dew of protection. When we D-O, God will send the D-E-W!!! When I did what God told me to do, the dew came.

This devotional *Just a Crumb* tool is just obedience to God. I put him first.

When you put him first, he will blow your mind. Stop putting your emotions first. Stop putting everyone else first. Stop putting what you feel needs to be first. Stop making excuses as to why you can't serve God, why you left the church, and why you don't give. You know God is real. You know God has been good to you. God is saying that what he has intentionally intended for you is being held up because you won't put him first. You know God has healed you, restored you, given you peace, given you joy, turned your life upside down, and you still put him second or third! Put God first and watch the D-E-W fall.

#justacrumb

#justacrumb

36

Day 7

Got Humility
James 4:6, 10

D o you remember back in the day when you would get some new sneakers or new jeans; and you got to go to school wearing your new gear (new sneakers and jeans)? You would know the humble ones because they wouldn't say anything about what they were wearing. Then there were the ones who had to bring attention to them. They would walk differently because their sneakers were so fresh that they wouldn't want to step in anything. They wouldn't sit in certain places because their jeans were so fresh. The humble ones didn't worry about that, and people would come and complement them. Only those who have no humility bring unnecessary attention to themselves.

So, I have a question.....Do *you* have humility?

Are you humble? Are you not thinking about yourself? You can always tell when someone is blessed by God by his humility. He's not proud or boastful. He's just humble. You may know people that have humility; and there are quite a few people who need humility. Some folks need a "taste of some humble pie" to bring them down to earth.

Sometimes we think we're all that, but we should remember that God resists the proud and gives grace to the humble. You can receive the blessings of God through your humility. Humility is the ability to be without pride or arrogance, and to know that God can do some amazing things in your life when you follow Him.

Some people are looking for God to do great, powerful, and awesome things in their lives, but they have no humility. They don't know how to humble themselves and to not think too highly of themselves. I want to encourage you to operate in humility. Great blessings, great miracles, and great open doors in your life come through humility -- when you learn not to think too highly of yourself or to promote yourself or to get on the bullhorn to bring attention to yourself. You should be humble. Humility goes a long way, sometimes things are not happening in your life because you have no humility.

Sometimes you might be looking for things to work out or for doors to open that don't open, and then someone comes along and says, "Humble yourself. You need some humility in your life."

I've seen a lot of people in my life be blessed just because of their humility. My father in ministry, Pastor John K. Jenkins, Sr., shows humility. God has done so much in his life because of his humility. He's a humble man, and through that, he's kind and generous.

God always blesses those who have some humility. I want to encourage you because you might be looking for some major things to happen in your life. Make sure that you're humble. Make sure you're level. Make sure you're easy. Make sure you follow God's plan for your life. Do what God has told you to do.

Jesus is the best example of someone who humbled Himself and followed God's plan for His life. Isn't it crazy? Isn't it amazing that even the Son of God operated with humility?

So, what makes you think that we shouldn't operate with humility?

Humility goes a long way. Humility is built and strengthened through your life experiences, through what you go through, through your ups and your downs. Humility is built through your challenge; it helps you to understand that you can't do this without God. Even in the tough times, it helps, especially when you know that you don't have enough money, enough education, or the pedigree to get yourself out of a situation, but you know how to humble yourself and that God can turn things around for you.

James 4:6 reads: "So humble yourselves before God. Resist the devil, and he will flee from you;" and James 4:10 reads: "Humble yourselves before the Lord, and he will lift you in honor." God resists the proud -- the ones that are always bragging and talking about themselves, the ones that always want all the attention for themselves. God resists those kinds of people. They're too proud. They're talking about themselves too much. They think they're the cat's meow and the dog's bow-wow. They think they're doing all kinds of things. God says he resists those people but lifts those who have humility. Humble yourself. When you humble yourself, He will lift you in honor.

Sometimes learning humility can be hard, because it breaks you down so that you know you're not all that. I know I'm not all that, nor do I claim to be. I don't need attention. I just wait for God to lift me.

I want to ask you this: "Got humility?" If you have got humility, God will do powerful things in your life and do things you never dreamed of or imagined. He will give you favor, honor, and understanding of who you are. A lot of people cannot understand who they are because they have no humility. You must humble yourself. You must be modest and meek. You need not think you're better than anyone else.

I want to encourage you to be humble and respect and honor authority, even if they are crazy and you know it. Do what you're supposed to do, and let humility give you honor. Even in drama, you need to humble yourself, and God will lift you. Some of you might be looking for ministry opportunities. Humble yourselves! Some doors have not opened for you because you're not humble. Some opportunities you're seeking have not presented themselves because you have no humility. "True humility and the fear of the Lord leads to riches, honor, and long life."

The Women's Basketball Head Coach for the University of

Connecticut Geno Auriemma said something interesting in an interview. Someone asked him how he picks the right people to be on his team, and how he determines when to play certain players. He said he watches their body language. He explained that he's not impressed with how they play. He said that he watches their body language in the game and their body language when they're on the bench. He said that he watches how they play, how they celebrate those who score, how they celebrate each other, how they encourage one another, how they say things to each other, how they pull the team together, and how they respond on the bench. He is looking for humility.

Some people are watching how you conduct yourself and what you're saying. They want to see how you respond when things are not going your way. They want to know if you can be encouraging to someone else.

"Humble yourself."

Humble yourselves before the Lord, and He will lift you in honor. People will recognize you and will say, "that's the person right there."

All Because You "Got Humility"

#justacrumb

#justacrumb

Day 8

Closed Mouth Won't Eat

Nehemiah 2:4-9

Once, when I was growing up as a young lad in the hood, I was hanging out all day with my father and I was hungry, but I didn't say anything. After a long day, my mother asked me, "Are you hungry?" And I said, "Yes ma'am." My father said, "Boy, you're hungry?" I said, "Yes." He said, "Boy, listen here… If you don't tell me, I don't know!" (Why is it that the fathers go through this?) I am going through that right now as a father. If I have been hanging out with my son, my wife can ask me, "Did you feed him (my son) today?" And I figure if the boy doesn't say anything, he's alright. I have to tell my son that if he's hungry, he has to tell me because a closed mouth won't eat.

Many of us go through life thinking that others know where we are or what we need. We sometimes believe that just walking past others allows them to sense that we require something. We think that they just need to see us to under-stand that we need help with something. Have you ever had someone in your house go out to the store after you get back from the same store? Have you ever said to that person, "Why didn't you tell me what you needed? I could have gotten that while I was at the store." It's like that.

You may be a person who has a dream and a vision for what you want to do in your life. There are people strategically placed around you, who can help you achieve your dream; but you have not said anything about it, so nobody knows what you need.

You won't eat. You can keep your mouth closed and miss out on major opportunities. When you don't indicate to anyone that you need help, direction, or insight, they won't ever know how you're feeling or what you're going through. A closed mouth won't eat.

You can go to work and not be feeling well, and someone could simply greet you, and you snap at them. The person replies, "What's wrong with you?" And you say that you're not having a good day. The person then says, "Well, how am I supposed to know that? You didn't say anything." Some of us have snapped at people and have thought someone else was supposed to read our body language. A closed mouth doesn't eat. Some of you want to start businesses, you want to travel, and; nobody knows or understands because you won't open your mouth.

I do a Morning Prayer call on social media, and I always ask people to share my broadcasts because I want more people to hear what God has given me to say. However, if I keep my mouth closed and never asks anyone to share; I defeat the purpose of going to social media in the first place. A closed mouth won't eat.

Nehemiah 2: 4-9, Look at what happens…

He begins to tell the king what he needs. He opens his mouth. If you don't open your mouth and express how you feel about something and express what's going on, no one will know. Even if you have opened your mouth and things didn't change, at least you're better off because you have expressed and shared what's on your heart. What is it that you want to do? What is your dream, your passion, your desire, your business? Nobody knows until you open your mouth. Nobody will hear until you open your mouth. A closed mouth will not eat. I want to encourage everyone to start opening your mouth. Stop keeping things silent. Stop walking around figuring somebody's going to read what you want to do, or that somebody's going to see what you want to do. No. Open your mouth.

When the Lord wakes you up in the morning, what's the one thing you hear outside? Birds! Birds are chirping to let you know, "We're alive and we're here." That's the same way you need to be. You've got to open your mouth, a closed mouth won't eat. You may have the ability, the gift, the talent, and the dream, but if you don't speak up, you should know that a closed mouth won't eat. If nobody knows what your dreams are, and nobody knows what your talents are, and nobody knows what you're trying to accomplish, and nobody knows where you're trying to go, or what business or ministry you want to start, or even what book you want to write, you will not achieve your goal.

So, my question is what is it that you want to do? What is your dream, your passion, your desire, your business? Nobody knows until you open your mouth. Nobody will hear until you open your mouth. A closed mouth will not eat. I want to encourage everyone to start opening your mouth. Stop keeping things silent. Stop walking around figuring some-body's going to read what you want to do, or that somebody's going to see what you want to do. No. Open your mouth.

Let people know about your dreams and what you want to do. I pray that God will put the right people in your path that will be a blessing to you because they heard about your dream. Back in the day, in our African American history, when a young one would want to go to college, Big Mama would put something in their hand and say, "Go get it." I encourage you to open your mouth and go get it!

#justacrumb

Day 9

What Are You Planting
Galatians 6:7

Growing up, I can recall my father's garden when we moved into our 1st home. I never planted a garden until my dad said, "We're going to plant a garden." He bought tools and everything to plant. I thought that all you had to do was get the seeds and throw them to the ground, but I learned that there was a preparation that needed to be done. The ground has to be prepared and tilled to get it smoothed out and to make sure it is ready to receive the seeds.

My father had cucumbers, peppers, tomatoes, green beans… all kinds of vegetables! It was awesome to plant and then see the vegetables come up! There was nothing like having fresh tomatoes, cucumbers, and peppers all from this garden. People would come to the house, and neighbors would ask, "What are you growing?" And then it turned into a whole neighborhood situation because others started growing their gardens with watermelons and all.

What God started speaking to me was that everybody can plant something. Everyone is some type of planter. You may not be a green thumb expert at knowing how to plant gardens and till the ground, but you can plant something. Everybody alive can plant something. The question is: Are you planting something to your flesh, or are you planting something spiritual?

A lot of us are always planting something. We all planned how we would go to the club. We planned what we would drink, who would drive what we would smoke, how we were going to hook up with somebody; and we also knew who could not be a part of the crew because they always messed up everything. We all planned what we were going to do because there was something we were going to plant.

We planned everything, even down to what we would do if things didn't work out well. The question is: Are you planting to the flesh or the spirit? If you are planting to the flesh, it may look good, feel good, sound good, smell good for a moment, but it won't last.

This preconceived notion that if we plant certain things they will last for a long time. Anytime you plant toward your flesh, it won't last. Everybody is a planter. We all can plant.

What you plant to your flesh won't last, but what you plant to your spirit will last for a long time. A lot of us have planted things to the flesh that we thought would be lasting, but it didn't last. When you gave your life to the Lord, you thought you could still hold onto some of the things you used to do. You wanted to know if you had to surrender everything. As soon as we said "yes" to the Lord, we tried to hold onto things we used to do, but it caused more drama, headaches, and issues because we tried to hold on and live for the Lord at the same time.

My question for you is: What are you planting? Are you planting to the flesh or the spirit?

You may wonder why the job and business aren't happening. It's because of what you're planting. If you plant defeat, you get defeat. If you plant a doubt, you get a doubt. If you plant "I can't do it," you get "I can't do it." As soon as you start planting the things of hope, of strength, of life, of good direction, and the right mindset, you will get a good harvest every time. So, what are you planting?

Who do you need to separate yourself from because they're still planting to their flesh? Is the reason you're getting no harvest that you are planting to the wrong thing? You're getting burnt out and worn out because you have too many things going on.

I had the opportunity to have one of my church family members with me for a day. I was pouring into his life. We hung out all day, and I asked him at one point if he needed to charge his phone. He told me that he didn't need a charger because he was in low power mode. I asked what that was. Low power mode helps to preserve your battery and it can help you as you go through your transactions, so that you don't have to keep charging. The battery holds its charge for a longer time in that mode. As soon as he told me about it, I did the same thing.

A lot of us waste a lot of energy because we are planting to things that are killing us and the stuff we are plugging into is sapping our strength. We are bringing about decay and things that don't give us strength.

Galatians 6:7, which says, "Don't be misled—you cannot mock the justice of God. You will always harvest what you plant. Those who live only to satisfy their sinful nature will harvest decay, and death from that sinful nature. But those who live to please the Spirit will harvest everlasting life from the Spirit." So, what are you planting? Are you planting to your flesh or are you planting to the spirit?

#justacrumb

Day 10

If You Don't Have Nothing Nice To Say Keep Your Mouth Shut
Proverbs 13:3

My mother used to tell me when I was a youngster, "Baby, if you don't have nothing nice to say, keep your mouth shut." In other words, what you can say can ruin things for people and yourself. Have you ever said something at a time where it got out too fast for you to catch it, and it jacked you up for the rest of the day, for the rest of the week, for the rest of the month because you said something that wasn't wholesome or positive?

There's an old proverb that says "words are like leaves in a storm" because, once you say them, it's hard to get them back. You can't retrieve them. Some of us have said things to people that we should not have said. We have said some things and someone was hurt or destroyed.

Or, you may have thought that what you said wouldn't come back, but it did. We must watch our mouths. If you don't have anything nice to say, keep your mouth shut. When my wife and I are talking, we sometimes keep our mouths shut because we know that we are going to say something that may not be helpful, wholesome, or positive.

We can see in the world around us how words can get people in trouble and cause them to feel the repercussions of something they have said. You have probably heard about Roseanne Barr, who said some racist comments in 2018 that got her show canceled, and jacked up everything and everybody that was working for her. Now, they don't have jobs anymore, all because she decided to say something that jacked up everything. The Bible is the truth. Whenever you open your mouth, you can jack everything up for everyone else and yourself. Roseanne opened her mouth and lost her job with no pay. They canceled everything. And everyone associated with her lost everything. They were guilty by association.

You have to watch your mouth. Do you know that when you say something out of place, it identifies your maturity? No, you need to keep your mouth shut. You can't say everything you want because it will come back to you. You must watch your mouth.

Whenever I would say something inappropriate, my mother would call me to the bathroom, and she would wash my mouth out with soap. Some of us need to have our mouths washed out with soap because we have said some things to people that we should not have said. And we need to understand that when we say things that are out of order, we are identifying the level of maturity we have. You should be mature enough not to say childish things or inappropriately say things.

Consider Proverbs 13:3, which states, "Those who control their tongue will have a long life; opening your mouth can ruin everything." In other words, you need to put that muscle, that powerful weapon in your mouth under control. You shouldn't say everything you think. Some of you need to pick up the phone, text, or Facetime folks to ask forgiveness because you have said something inappropriate or out of order. It shows your level of maturity.

You must make sure that what you say is mature. You can say what you want to say. That's not the world we live in. Back in the day, you would get a fat lip for what you would say.

If you have already said something that was out of bounds, foul, or inappropriate, it is okay to call the ones you have offended. The Bible says that those who control the tongue will have a long life. Opening your mouth can ruin everything.

My niece/goddaughter has a chore. During the week, she must clean the kitchen, sweep the floor, etc. So, my goddaughter must do these chores. On one particular day, she had a lot of help. Instead of being done in 15 minutes, she was done in over an hour. Some of you need to watch your mouths because it's prolonging your productivity. Nothing is getting accomplished because you're running your mouth. Some of you are missing out on blessings because you're running your mouth too much.

The Bible says those who control their tongue will have a long life. Opening your mouth can ruin it. Let's be mature and be observant and notice what we're saying, what we're talking about. Let's be mindful of that.

#justacrumb

#justacrumb

Day 11

Someone Is Always Watching
Colossians 4:5, 6

If you are in a crowded room if you are at an event or even if you are just out and about, someone is always watching or observing you. Even if you are in a room of 500 people, someone will notice you there. Isn't it amazing that out of so many people someone sees you? They notice your hair, your hat, your walk... That's why it is so important that we watch how we behave. Somebody is always paying attention. Not only are they always watching you, but they are always listening to you, too.

Young people are more observant of us today than they were 30 years ago. And they are inquisitive, too. So, you cannot just say what you want and do what you want; and you have to be careful where you go because someone is always watching and listening.

Have you ever done something out in public that you thought you got away with only for someone to tell you later that they saw you in that place? You start to replay all of your actions in that place, don't you? If you are always careful to act appropriately, you do not have to worry about situations like this one.

Colossians 4:5-6: "Live wisely among those who are not believers. Let your conversation be gracious and attractive so that you will have the right response for everyone."

A lot of times the people who are watching you and listening to you are not believers, especially if you claim the name of Jesus. You have to be mindful of what you are saying and doing and ensure that you always have the right responses. Someone is always watching or listening.

 Remember to represent the King of Kings and the Lord of Lords correctly and let God do what he does best.

#justacrumb

#justacrumb

Day 12

Unlearn What You Have Learned
2 Kings 5:5-15

Anybody that knows me knows that I love Stars Wars, written and directed by George Lucas. I think the movies have been phenomenal! I go to see them all. One of my favorite characters in Stars Wars is Master Yoda. He is the master Jedi. Luke goes to Master Yoda to get trained to be a full-fledged Jedi Knight. When Luke is in training, his ship sinks into the swamp and he has to get it out. He doesn't know how to get it out, and Yoda is trying to get Luke to raise the ship out of the swamp. Luke, who had been able to move stones using the force before, thinks it is impossible to lift the ship and says "moving stones is one thing, but this is a ship." Yoda says, "So certain, are you?" Then he says, "You have to unlearn what you have learned."

What do you need to accomplish that might require you to unlearn what you have learned? Whenever you're trying to progress, excel, get ahead, or obtain something you need, you may have to unlearn what you have learned. In other words, you can't get what you need if you keep doing what you've been doing or keep using the same mentality. Somewhere down the line, you have to unlearn what you have learned. You have to do something that different that will bring about change in your life.

Some of us are doing the same thing over and over and need a breakthrough: a new job, some money, a better doctor's report, some help in school. You may need a lot of things, but you will need to unlearn what you have learned. You will have to stop thinking, acting, talking, behaving the way you always have, and saying the same things you have been. A lot of times we can't learn something new because we are resistant to doing something new. It's kind of like rejecting the instruction of your parents, who tell you to, "Just do what I told you to do." What is it that you need to stop resisting?

2 King 5-15. This passage is about Namaan, a gentile commander of the Syrian army. He is a prestigious, decorated warrior, but he has a problem: leprosy. In one battle, he acquired a young girl who became the maid in his home,

and she, seeing Namaan's problem, said, "if only my master would go to the prophet in Israel, he would be healed." So, Namaan goes to his King and asks him for a letter that he can take to the King of Israel to request that he be healed of his leprosy.

Elijah hears that Namaan is coming, and sends his servant to tell Namaan to dip himself in the Jordan River seven times. Namaan questions the instructions. He hears the instructions, but he is resistant. Some of us are like Namaan, we are too resistant and that prevent us from unlearning what we have learned. We ask why a lot. We have so many questions, comments, and reasons why we won't do anything, and nothing changes in our lives.

Don't miss this Namaan has a problem, but he is resistant. He doesn't want to change. He wanted to go into another river: a cleaner one, one that was more prestigious, one that would allow him to be seen, that would show his greatness. Some of us resemble Namaan. We want people to see us, but we need to humble ourselves.

Namaan has a selfish response. He thinks that Elijah should wave his hand over him, but instead, he instructs Namaan to do something uncomfortable. Some of you are on the brink of accomplishing so much, but you have so many excuses. God is asking, "When are you going to do what I told you to do?"

Some of us miss out on the blessings of God because we won't unlearn what we've learned. Some of us can go beyond where we are, but we are intimidated and think we might show somebody up, lose friends, or be unpopular with people. Don't worry about that. You've got this. You are hindering yourself and others all because you have a selfish response.

But, Namaan's servant tells him that he would not have been resistant to Elijah's instructions had he been told to do something popular, difficult, or more challenging. Namaan's servant was baffled because all Namaan had to do was dip himself in the Jordan to get what he needed.

So, what do you have to unlearn to get your breakthrough? As soon as Namaan did what the man of God told him to do, he was restored. He moved from resistant, to a selfish response, to listening to the reasoning of his servant, to finally get restoration.

If you are still doing the same thing you've done and have not followed God's simple instructions, if you are being resistant, you should unlearn what you have learned and do what God has told you to do.

BILLY T. STATON, JR.

#justacrumb

#justacrumb

Day 13

Dry Seasons
Ezekiel 37:1-3a

Summers in DC, MD, VA, or the DMV as it is affectionately called by those raised in this area are some crazy Hot/Humid Days that bring some devastating "Dry Seasons" lawns that are dry and yellow HVAC systems working overtime trying to keep everyone cool swimming pools are jammed packed. The Hot/Humid summer that brings about these "Dry Seasons" could last some days or some months. This can make it very uncomfortable and unhealthy where breathing and allergies can be very challenging. The one thing that can change "Dry Seasons" is when God allows a good rain to come that brings life to our lawns and removes the pollen so people can breathe and be comfortable and the electric bill goes down.

Sometimes in life, business, ministry, we experience a dry season. Have you ever had the challenge of a dry season? It is a period in your life where it seems like nothing is working right and there's one problem after another. You may have great expectations, but then issues arise. You think you're progressing in your marriage, in your finances, in your health; but for some reason, it's a dry season. Every time you turn around, something is happening that you didn't anticipate.

"Dry Seasons" feel like nothing is being produced. Everything is just Dry -- marriage, career, relationships -- it's just dry. Dry seasons are frustrating but are a necessary part of our growth. So the question is, "What can you do in a dry season?"

I want to encourage you to have a consistent connection with God that allows God to show you or tell you what you need to do. Sometimes we are in a dry season because we are not doing what God told us to do. God may have told us to move forward on something, to stop something, or to go somewhere; but because we have not done what he told us, we are stuck. And the funny thing is that we are trying to figure out why we are in a dry season, and it's all because we have not listened to God. We have not followed his instructions. Following God's instructions is critical to escaping the dry season.

Ezekiel 37 the word of God declares, "The Lord took hold of me, and I was carried away by the Spirit of the Lord to a valley filled with bones. He led me all around among the bones that covered the valley floor. They were scattered everywhere across the ground and were completely dried out. Then he asked me, "Son of man, can these bones become living people again?" (Ezekiel 37:1-3a)

Look at what God does. The spirit of God leads Ezekiel to a valley of dry bones, and then he asks him the question, "Can these dry bones live again?" I believe God is asking a lot of us this question right now. He is asking: "Can your marriage live again?" "Can your finances live again?" "Can your career live again?" "Can your ministry breathe again?" Many of us are experiencing Dry Seasons in our lives and God is asking if these things can live again.

"Dry Seasons" can turn for the better when you speak what God has told you to say. God told Ezekiel what to speak to the dryness, and God has given you a word -- not your own opinion, not your thoughts, not your insights -- to speak to your dry season.

God is saying all you have to do is speak to the dry areas of your life and let the word of God be strength and hope for you. Speak the word of God. Speak truth to your Dry Seasons. Speak it! you will live and not die, that you are the head and not the tail, that you are above only, that the Lord has given you power, that the Lord is your shepherd, that you should be anxious for nothing. Speak the word to your family, to your health challenges, to your finances, to your career, to your ministry, to all of the drama, and to the places where you have no direction. God is showing us through this communication with Ezekiel that we simply need to follow instructions and speak the word.

Once you have spoken to your situation, you might think that the change is coming overnight or in the next couple of hours, or momentarily. That's not necessarily so. What you should understand is that you have the authority to speak to your situation now. The timing of your change is on God. All he needs you to do is maintain your connection with him and speak the word. Speak what he gives you to say and wait and watch God give you strength, encouragement, peace, and joy.

BILLY T. STATON, JR.

#justacrumb

#justacrumb

Day 14

Purpose
Judges 13-16

Everyone who is born has a purpose, which can be best fulfilled by surrendering to God. You may think that something you do well is your purpose, but maybe that's not it. It could just be a vehicle to get you to your purpose. I thought my purpose was basketball, but even basketball got cut short. I can play, of course, and I love the game; but the game is not why I am here. I used to think it was. Then I said to myself, Okay, I'm a musician and I will be a professional musician. But it was right in the middle of my professional musicianship that someone saw me and told me that music was not my purpose. I was playing the drums, and out of nowhere, the Lord sent a woman of God to tell me that playing drums was not my purpose. God reminded me at that point that my purpose was related to something that I had been running from and avoiding, something that I had first done when I was 12 years old when I first opened the word of God before people.

There was one point at my church where I was teaching a lot about living a life that is fully surrendered to God -- fully yielded to the authority of God in your life. When you have surrendered to God, which means that God has everything. It is a challenge to fully surrender because that means you are giving him total control, that you are not making a move without consulting him. That's why prayer and fasting are important. Praying and fasting allow you to hear God. When your life is fully surrendered, you can hear God and know how he speaks. He doesn't just speak in an audible voice, but he can speak through family, circumstances, your money, your health, and many other ways.

So many of us have been running, because we don't want to fully surrender to God. But doing your purpose means that there is something that God has put something in you that you must do. It's something that you know beyond a shadow of a doubt. End So many people end up doing things that are totally outside of the will of God because they don't want to surrender, but you have an opportunity to embrace the purpose that God has given you. You simply have to surrender and give God full control. You have to tell him that you're going to give him everything.

Judges 13-16 tells us the story of Samson. Samson was born with a purpose. His mother was informed by an angel of the Lord that she would have a child whose head could not be shaved, who could not eat anything unclean, and who would be used to fight against the Philistines. He would be the champion. But for a time, Samson was not reaching the full potential of his purpose because he was not fully surrendered to God. When you read the story, you see that he has a purpose, but he detours and tells riddles to people and connects with people that he shouldn't. He seems like the "big dog", but he is not fulfilling the purpose for his life.

Samson then connects with a woman of Timnah, who is a pagan worshipper from outside of his culture. His parents wonder why he wants this woman, but he insists on marrying her. Every step he makes is not in line with his purpose. It's not until Chapter 16 that he fulfills his purpose. It is at this point that he gets connected with Delilah, who is a smooth criminal with one agenda -- to snatch the gift that he has. It is not until his eyes are burned out and he is in chains that he fulfills his purpose.

What is your purpose? Why does God have you here? You know what it is. And the purpose is best fulfilled when you are fully surrendered to God. I had to learn that because I was trying to do me. I wanted to play drums. I wanted to play basketball. But neither of those was my purpose. I have the talent to do those things, but my purpose is to do what I am doing now. When I finally took my hands off, yielded to God, surrendered to him, gave him full control, life has been so much better. Is it sometimes challenging? Yes, it is. The challenge helps to develop you, build you up, and equip you.

You have a purpose. It is time for you to fulfill it. Why are you here? You have to be fully committed to God so that you can make a difference. Read about Samson in Judges Chapters 13-16. It wasn't until he died in chapter 16:28, which says, "Then Samson prayed to the Lord, 'Sovereign Lord, (now he's talking to the Lord where we never hear him talk to the Lord in the previous chapters, although he should have been doing that a long time ago)..." It is time for you to step into whatever it is that God has told you to do. It's not hard. What's hard is letting go of you. What's hard is trusting in the Lord with all your heart and leaning not to your understanding, in all your ways acknowledging him and allowing him to direct your path (Proverbs 3:5-6). When you trust in the Lord with all your heart, you are fully surrendered to God. When

I trust him and am surrendered to him, he has full control. It means that I am taking my hands off and letting him work out what it is that he has placed inside of me.

God did not create you to take up space, but to fulfill a purpose. Everybody is born with a purpose, and it is time for you to fulfill yours. You can't wing it. You're winging it when you're not surrendered.

#justacrumb

84

#justacrumb

Day 15

He Is My Shepherd
Psalm 23:1-6

My wife doesn't like crowds, whenever we are somewhere together and there is a crowd coming, I can extend my hand and she grabs it not just because of what she sees but because of what she senses. I can see what she senses, and as long as we are going through and she is holding my hand tight, everything is alright. You may be going through rough terrain, and you will make it through as long as you stick with the shepherd. My wife is okay because she stays connected to the leader. If you are not connected to the leader, you need to get connected.

Psalm 23 is the Bible verse of all Bible verses. I believe that throughout history Psalm 23 has been the Bible verse to beat all Bible verses. I recall that in ministry, even as a youth pastor, Psalm 23 was read often. People have always seemed to want to hear the old King James Version. It's a powerful, declarative psalm because it is saying that the Lord is my shepherd. And I believe that if he is your shepherd, then you have to belong to him. That means that you have confessed Him as Lord and that you are fully surrendered to him. That means you will not hear the voice of a stranger. It means you are not easily detoured and that you are following him as he leads.

So many of us want to claim that God is ours, but we haven't fully surrendered and yielded to him. We have not committed our lives to him, but we want the perks. When you say that he is your shepherd, you have truly committed and surrendered your life to him. It means that he is in full control. When you say he is my shepherd, it is much more powerful. You are saying, Lord, I belong to you and have committed my life and way to you.

When God is your shepherd, He makes sure you have provisions. There's nothing you need that you don't have. You allow him to guide and direct you. Not only do you have his provision, but you have his protection. When you go through

rough terrain (the shepherd may take you places that could be a little rough), you are indeed going through.

The shepherd gives protection. He also has a rod and a staff. He has a rod to put the sheep back in line and a staff to get the sheep out of sticky situations. Some of us getting into sticky situations, but the shepherd have the right tools to pull us out every time. I am grateful for God being my shepherd with a staff who can save me every time. He is my provision, my protection, and my power.

Only my shepherd has the power to prepare a table in the presence of my enemies. And he anoints my head with oil -- oil for the soothing of scratches, scrapes, and wounds. The Bible does not tell us that when he is our shepherd we will have no wounds. The fact is that you will get wounds in the valley, but he will anoint your head with oil and set you apart in the presence of your enemies.

He lays a spread and my cup runs over. When I was a kid and would visit with my grandparents, my grandfather would drink coffee with a saucer. He would pour his coffee in the cup and the coffee would run over into the saucer. He would be there eating his grits, his eggs, his red hot toast and sipping on his coffee. After finishing his cup of coffee, he would drink the overflow from the saucer.

All I am trying to say is when you declare that he is your shepherd; he will make sure you have provision, protection, and power. He's got the power to prepare a table for you in the presence of your enemies and to anoint your head with oil. When he's your shepherd, you will let him lead and protect. You will not live or speak any kind of way. You will know that he has the power to turn everything around! Let's live the way God tells us to live, and we will have an overflow; he will make sure everything is good for you. Do you understand that? When you allow God to be your shepherd, he gives provision, protection, and power that can bring things into your life and allow blessings to overtake you.

You get friends. Surely goodness and mercy will follow you all the days of your life, and even when you get to glory, it's permanent. You will be with him in the house of the Lord forever.

#justacrumb

#justacrumb

Day 16

Encourage Others
Roman 12:15, 16

I once went shopping for some sneakers and, as I was leaving the store, I saw a sister in the faith who told me that she had just gotten a promotion. I was excited for her, and my reaction must have surprised her because she thought I seemed maybe a little too happy. But I had to tell her that I truly was excited for her and was thanking God for what he was doing for her. I told her that she didn't know what was coming my way, and I was thanking God for what was getting close in my own life. She didn't know what I had been praying about or looking for God to do.

Do you know that when others are being blessed, you have to learn how to celebrate with them? That means God is in the neighborhood! I have a brother who had an excellent performance evaluation and a raise in his job. I was excited for him and celebrated with him. When God is doing something in someone else's life, you have to learn to celebrate with them. You have to learn to cheer them. There is no need to be upset because it just shows that God is close by. He is in the neighborhood, and he might stop at your house next.

Our problem is so often that we don't know how to celebrate others. We are supposed to rejoice with those who are going through good times; and even in the hard times, we have to be there to encourage and put a smile on someone's face. No matter what is happening in your life, learn to celebrate, and be with those who are going through good times and rough times. I am just learning this whole process of celebrating others' accomplishments and how God is blessing them. Even if they look at you funny, celebrate them. I was so happy about how God blessed my sister in the faith, and then I heard from my brother! Double celebration!

When you hear that God is blessing someone, when he has performed a miracle, when he has changed someone's situation, don't keep your mouth shut. Scream from the mountaintops what God is doing in someone else's life. Whenever he does something for someone else, you are close to your breakthrough.

Romans 12:15-16 which says, "Be happy with those who are happy, and weep with those who weep. Live in harmony with each other. Don't be too proud to enjoy the company of ordinary people. And don't think you know it all!"

That means to have joy with those who have joy and be there for those who are going through a hard time. Be consistent. Don't act funny with people. Be easy, relaxed, and calm. You should be celebrating somebody. Everyone needs that now and then. Did you encourage somebody today? Did you pray for somebody today? Did you encourage somebody who felt down today?

I am proud of you and celebrate you, your victories, and how God is lifting you. I also ask for God's blessings on you in your hard times. He will be right there with you, and your hard times will not last forever. Remember that weeping may endure for a night, but joy is coming in the morning. God is sending his help in your direction. I celebrate what God is doing in your life!

When God is in the neighborhood and is closer than you could ever imagine. You may have been praying, fasting, and seeking God for a right-now blessing, and I want to encourage you. He is about to bless you. You are about to be upgraded.

God is upgrading your faith, your joy, your strength, your life, your family life, your marriage. Everything about you is getting upgraded. God is going to blow your mind. Just be happy and encourage others.

BILLY T. STATON, JR.

#justacrumb

#justacrumb

Day 17

Please You More
Ephesians 4:1-3

Recently I was working out at my gym and the Lord began to speak to me through a song by one of my favorite groups, Commissioned. The song is called "Please You More". We should want God to be proud of how we're living. We should want to live a life that pleases God more. How can we please God more? What can we do to bring him more honor, glory, and praise? We could love, be kind to one another and go the extra mile for one another, but there is more we can do.

Ephesians 4:1-3 is a powerful passage of scripture that speaks to how we can please God more. The passage reads, "Therefore I, a prisoner for serving the Lord, beg you to lead a life worthy of your calling, for you have been called by God. Always be humble and gentle. Be patient with each other, making allowance for each other's faults because of your love. Make every effort to keep yourselves united in the Spirit, binding yourselves together with peace."

This passage highlights being humble; and humility means putting Christ first, putting someone else second, and putting yourself last. It is the understanding that it's not about you. God is looking for people to be humble, especially in the household of faith. Putting God first, people second, and you last are a servant's attitude. It is a godly thing.

Have you ever met someone with no humility? They think they're all that. Those kinds of people are dangerous because they're not prepared for hardship. When you practice humility, you can, for example, put another person ahead of you in the grocery line. God always honors that type of humility, and it is a way to please him more.

Being gentle is having power under control. It is not a form of weakness, but strength. The Lord wants us to have power under control. Having gentleness understands that you could, in some situations, respond in a not-so-gentle manner. You could set some things and some people straight, and folks around you are encouraging you to do just that, but you decide to have power under control so that you do not damage another individual or yourself. You don't want to disrupt everything and mess up God's flow and blessings in your life because somebody said something wrong to you and you didn't exercise control.

In Ephesians 4, God is also telling us to learn patience, to calm down and relax. God is saying that he was patient with you, he was gentle with you. Why can't you be patient with someone else? You must have some longsuffering, some endurance. You must be able to deal with people.

When you let the word saturate you and take control of you, it will bring about a flavor and fragrance in your life that is very powerful. You can then say that it is not you, but that you allowed the word to guide your thinking, your speech, and your approach to life. You can say that it has caused more patience and humility and that you have learned to make an allowance for another's faults. You can say that you have learned to love even difficult people. There are difficult people all over -- in your family, in the church, in the community. You have to love them, even if they have done something unbecoming. What helps and delivers people is love. You have to go the extra mile and love them. People make mistakes; they do things that are not the greatest. Loving others builds character.

99

Pleasing God means that you have to be humble, gentle, patient, and make allowances for others. It requires that you make the effort to go the extra mile and go beyond what anyone could imagine or expect from you. You have to work at it. Sometimes it isn't a one-shot deal. You may have to keep being humble, gentle, and patient. You have to be intentional to ensure you are all that God wants you to be.

Day 18

Saying T. H. A. N. K. Y. O. U.

Proverbs 23:7; Psalm 66:19, 20; 1Tim.2:5, 6
Hebrews 13:5; Isaiah 26:3; Psalm139:7-12
James 4:8; Psalm 145:18; Ephesians 3:20

When I was a youngster my mother and father taught me always to be respectful. You know what I'm speaking of to say yes and no ma'am and yes and no sir but there's one that I will always remember and that is don't nobody have to be nice or kind to me so I should always say Thank You. So, I felt led to mention to you all who are reading this to remind you to say Thank You to our God. But, here's something to consider when you're saying Thank You to God I hope it encourages you and reminds you why we should say Thank You!!!

T - Teacher. I want to thank God for being a teacher to me. He has helped me to think better, to speak better, and to be better. Sometimes I had stinking thinking, but he helped me. I want to thank him for helping me be better at thinking through teaching me to embrace Proverbs 23:7 (as a man thinks so is he). I want to thank God for just being a teacher and helping me in every area of my life. Just like he has helped me in the area of my life, he can help you, too.

H - Hearer. God is also a hearer and always listens to my prayers. You may have been praying some prayers that have not been answered, but he hears and he knows exactly what he's doing. Don't be defeated or discouraged. He will do it in his time, not your time. Consider Psalm 66:19-20, which reads, "But God did listen! He paid attention to my prayer. Praise God, who did not ignore my prayer or withdraw his unfailing love from me." God is paying attention and always has a listening ear. I want to encourage you to never stop praying. He is always listening. Never stop praying. Don't stop. He hears. You have been praying for a loved one, your children, your spouse, a new job, the government, our country. I want you to know that he hears your prayers.

A - Advocate. The Lord is an advocate. He steps in and says "Father, forgive them for they know not what they do." 1

Timothy 2:5-6 tells us, "There is one God and one Mediator who can reconcile God and humanity—the man Christ Jesus. He gave his life to purchase freedom for everyone. This is the message God gave to the world at just the right time." The Lord gave his life to purchase freedom for everyone. He is your advocate. He steps in and speaks on your behalf. Even when you deserve to be spanked, to be punished, he steps in and advocates for you. He makes sure that what should have wiped you out does not wipe you out.

N - Never neglects. The Lord never leaves me hanging. He never abandons me, and he will never abandon you. The family may leave when things get tough, but God stays with you. Hebrews 13:5 states "Don't love money; be satisfied with what you have. For God has said, 'I will never fail you. I will never abandon you.'" This is why we can cast all of our cares upon him. He cares for you. He will never leave you.

K - Keeper. The Lord is a keeper. He keeps my mind, my body, and my family intact. He can do the same for you. Even when there are all kinds of situations happening in your life, he will keep you in perfect peace. Isaiah 26:3 states, "You will keep in perfect peace, all who trusts in you, all whose thoughts are fixed on you!" He is a keeper! He knows how to keep you on the straight and narrow.

Y - You are always there. You never leave me nor forsake me. Psalm 139:7-12 (can never escape...). Every time I look, you are there. I can go to the lowest points in my life and you are always there.

O - Open the door. The Lord gives you access. You have 24/7 access to him 365 days of the year...366 in a leap year! Psalm 145:18 states, "The Lord is close to all who call on him, yes, to all who call on him in truth." James 4:8 says, "Come close to God, and God will come close to you..." All you have to do is come close to God. He is always there, and you have access to him. He has an open-door policy.

U - Unlimited. God is unlimited in love, kindness, power, provision, mercy, truth, strength, and protection. God is unlimited! Ephesians 3:20 gives us insight into the Lord's unlimited power by stating, "Now to Him who is able to do exceedingly abundantly above all that we ask or think..." Remember that you have access to our God who has unlimited power.

So, Let's Clear our throats and minds and just "THANK YOU" to the one who has made everything possible, better, and stronger!!!

BILLY T. STATON, JR.

#justacrumb

#justacrumb

Day 19

Stay In the Pocket
Proverbs 3:5, 6

My son Benjamin is an awesome musician, and to be a great musician he is learning to always stay in the pocket. I'm always telling the Producers to see the difference between good and great musicians are the one who stays in the pocket. The pocket is the place where the groove is. With God, the pocket is the place where you understand his rhythm, his timing, his cadence. Some of you are looking for God to do something in your life, but God just wants you to be in the pocket. So many of us started in the pocket with God but then got out of the pocket.

Do you know how some of us get out of the pocket? It is when God gives us what we have been praying for. We get it, and then we forget what he's done. We stop praying, reading our Bible, serving in ministry and so many other things.

Proverbs 3:5-6: "Trust in the Lord with all your heart; do not depend on your own understanding. Seek his will in all you do, and he will show you which path to take."

You may have fallen out of pocket because you have been depending on your thinking and your understanding. You stopped trusting God. Your thinking has taken the driver's seat. The problem is that your thinking gets you in trouble. You have to trust in God with all of your heart and let Him lead and guide you. You have to stay in the pocket with him.

God has been helping you for a long time. He did something no one else could do, but you have fallen out of the pocket. You may have gotten a bad report from the doctor or you may have lost your job. You may even be struggling without enough money. Things are helter-skelter in your life, but that is only because you have not stayed in the pocket with God. You have to trust in the Lord. Get back to your prayer time. Get back to your quiet time. You used to fast. Go back to the pocket. Go back to praying, reading your word, doing ministry. You may have been involved in major outreach. Stay in the pocket. A pocket is a place where there is a sustained groove. There are rhythm and a tempo in the pocket that never ceases.

#justacrumb

Day 20

Be Consistent
Matthew 5:37

Recently, I have been on a weight loss journey, and it has been incredible. I love it! My face is starting to shrink and my wife even told me that she could finally see my ears. Ha! I love the challenge and the different things that I do, but what makes it significant is that I am consistent.

I don't like the cold, so working out in the cold outside was a problem for me. Someone told me, however, to dress in layers, and that advice allowed me to avoid inconsistency in my workout. I think we hinder ourselves and fall short of our goals because we are not consistent in anything -- at work, to our families. We are inconsistent because an excuse arises that hinders us from being consistent.

I remember how I used to work out and take care of myself before this weight loss journey. I was going to the gym before, but I looked for reasons (for excuses) to be inconsistent. If you are expecting a breakthrough in your life, if you are expecting something to turn around in your life, you have to be consistent. You can be effective over time if you're consistent, but you have to ask yourself, "What can I do to be more consistent?" When you're inconsistent, it leaves room for excuses: "My head hurts," "my shoulder hurts," "I'm not feeling it today."

I want to encourage you to be consistent in your prayer life, in your study time, in your giving, in loving people, in serving people, and in trusting God. When you are inconsistent, you miss out and have to start over again. You leave too much room for excuses. Be consistent in your marriage, with your family, with your finances, in your health, and your faith. When you stop being consistent, that's when everything turns upside down.

Matthew 5:37, which states, "But let your 'Yes' be 'Yes,' and your 'No,' No.'

For whatever is more than these are from the evil one." It is important to just say a simple "Yes, I will" or "No, I won't."

The evil one always presents inconsistency, excuses, and the "I can't do it" mentality. Just do what you say you are going to do, otherwise you're inconsistent. If you're going to walk with the Lord, be consistent. If you're going to pray or serve others, be consistent. Many of us cannot get to our goals because we are inconsistent. We start well but end up with difficulty. Are you going to be consistent and do what God is telling you to do?

Chick-fil-A understands consistency. I don't care where you go in the country or the world, every time you enter a Chick-fil-A; they begin with a consistent greeting: "Good morning/afternoon/evening, welcome to Chick-fil-A. How can I serve you?" And Chick-fil-A benefits from providing a consistently positive and pleasant experience for customers. It is mind-blowing! If we are consistent in all that we do, God will blow our minds. He is prepared to do it.

You might say that you tried God and it didn't work out; but did you make the effort to go the extra mile? Chances are you were looking for a way to be inconsistent for one reason or another. As soon as you decide in your heart and mind to be consistent, things will change. You have to step out of the box of mediocrity, of doubting yourself, of low self-esteem, of low confidence, and step into the water of consistency. Then, when you get into the groove of consistency, go for it! Be consistent!

#justacrumb

#justacrumb

Day 21

It Ain't About You
Galatians 11

So often, people perceive that life is all about them. Some of us think we're the cat's meow and the dog's bow-wow. It's not about you. Sometimes you are being changed, set free, or delivered for someone else. That means that everything you are doing is not just for you. You should be glad to have been reformed, inspired, and healed, but that is all for someone that has not experienced the love of Christ, someone that has low self-esteem, no purpose, or no direction. You are to share with someone else and be encouraging to someone else.

Your salvation is not for you. It is for you to tell someone else what God has done. We often think that surrendering our lives was to make us better. While that's true, you have to understand that surrendering to him and submitting to his word allows him to use you to serve others and share what he has done in your life. So, this salvation thing is just not for you.

I'm glad about being saved, healed, and delivered, but it wasn't all for me. It's for the one I may meet on the subway, in my travels. The change in your life is not for you, but for the next person who is lost, who is going through trials. It is for the person who sits two cubicles over. It's for the one who comes to work depressed. That person is the reason God has delivered you and cleaned you up. Your salvation is to help someone else understand God's love and that he can change anybody.

Ephesians 3:1 where Paul says, "When I think of all this, I, Paul, a prisoner of Christ Jesus for the benefit of you Gentiles ..." Paul goes back to the time of his conversion and remembers what he used to do -- how he persecuted the church and shut them down. Galatians 1:11-24 says, "Dear brothers and sisters, I want you to understand that the gospel message I preach is not based on mere human reasoning. I received my message from no human source, and no one taught me. Instead, I received it by direct revelation from Jesus Christ.

You know what I was like when I followed the Jewish religion—how I violently persecuted God's church. I did my best to destroy it. I was far ahead of my fellow Jews in my zeal for the traditions of my ancestors. But even before I was born, God chose me and called me by his marvelous grace. Then it pleased him to reveal his Son to me so that I would proclaim the Good News about Jesus to the Gentiles." Paul is saying that God chose him and he understood that it was not about him.

This salvation is not about us, and it is critical we understand that. It is about the folks who have not heard about or experienced Jesus. It is about the ones who have not latched on or even heard the good news that Jesus died, was buried, rose ascended to the father, and is coming back. That's what it's about! Your job, your money, your house, your car is not about you. It is about you being used by God to be a blessing to someone else that needs love, encouragement, motivation… Who have you spoken to at your job, at your favorite store -- Wegmans, Target, Wal-Mart? Who have you connected to that someone would hear the good news of Jesus Christ?

Wherever you go, it's not about you. Even if you are working out, you should be hoping that God will set you up so you can share the gospel of Jesus Christ. If you're married, it's not about you. You have to draw strength from God to learn how to love your spouse unconditionally, to care for your spouse, to pray for your spouse. We are in covenant with Jesus Christ and he loves us despite our imperfections, shortcomings, or our going astray. That's the relationship we have with him.

Paul says that when he thinks of how God has delivered and saved and changed and healed him, he is a prisoner of Jesus Christ. He was in prison for loving and encouraging Gentiles. He did not get saved just to be able to tell others he was saved or delivered. Jesus saved us so that we could live our lives telling others about the good news, to tell others that if he did it for us, he could do it for them, too.

If you're in church leadership, it's not about you. It's about living life in a way that people are compelled to come closer and they allow you to speak about your surrender to God and how that allows you to serve and share with someone else. What God has done in your life is not for you. It is for you to be a giver of what he's done for you. You have to give to somebody else what he gave you -- love, peace, another chance.

Even believers sometimes need to hear some encouraging words, a prayer, something to keep us moving forward. My spiritual daughter told a story about how she witnessed to another believer. She thanked God for her ability to pray with someone else and to share with and encourage another person.

Let the glory of God be unleashed. May the Lord be with you. And may he keep you constantly reminded that it's not about you!

#justacrumb

Day 22

God Is Able
Ephesians 3:20

I once heard a relevant story about two fishermen: one of them was having no luck catching fish on his side of the river. The other one was catching everything on his side but was throwing back the big fish. When asked why he was throwing back the big fish, the man explained that it was because they wouldn't fit in his small pan. Many of us have a small pan mentality and small pan speech. If you are one of those people, you have to get around those who talk and think big. You have to understand that you serve a God who can do more than you can ask or think according to the power of the Holy Spirit that works in you. You just have not tapped into the power because of our small mindset and speech. What have you stopped asking God? What are you looking for God to do? Whatever it is, he's able. He is able to do exceedingly; abundantly above all you can ask or think.

So often in our lives, we stop praying and believing that God can handle our situations, and we take matters into our own hands. We short change God with our thinking and our speech. We think with a small mindset and our speech indicates that mindset. We talk, think, and believe small. We say things that don't make sense, not understanding that God operates often on what we say. We often fail to consider

Ephesians 3:20: "Now to Him who is able to do exceedingly abundantly above all that we ask or think, according to the power that works in us..." God can do things beyond what we can think or ask. Paul, here, is talking about a God who is able to do things that exceed and surpass, that go above and beyond anything we can think. All you have to do is think big.

Know that God is able...period! He is able to restore, to heal, and to give life, to turn things around, to make things better, and to bring things to a screeching halt. He is able to bring you out of darkness into light. Whatever you are thinking... he is able to do; and he is able to go beyond whatever you ask or think. For every situation and every challenge, he is able. God is able to heal your marriage. God is able to heal your financial situation, to restore you, to give life, and to give strength. You have to stop coming with a small pan mentality and believe God.

Sometimes, you have to take pictures of what you want God to do. Recently, I took a picture of something that later became mine. When I took a picture, it materialized quickly. I wasn't even thinking that God would do what he did.

You have to keep dreaming and go large. Your photos and your writing things down are your asking and thinking, but you have to ask and think big for things you have never dreamed or imagined. God is able.

Think big! Talk big! Take pictures. Write it down. Believe God because his word says that he is able to do exceedingly, abundantly above all that we ask or think according to the power that works in you. To him be all glory…

God is able. When you think big, talk big, and take pictures, you can't hang with the same folks anymore. Some are not thinking big, talking big, or taking pictures. They are just complaining. They are in the same circles and the same posture. They are not looking to do anything huge. They have a crab and a small pan mentality. The crab mentality means that they want you to stay with them. Always believe God Is Able!!!

#justacrumb

#justacrumb

Day 23

Hold Onto God
Psalm73:26

Hold onto God no matter what. Don't let go. In the end, he will bless you real good!

Psalm 73:26, which says "My health may fail, and my spirit may grow weak, but God remains the strength of my heart; he is mine forever."

Even if you go through circumstances, problems, situations, issues, pain, ensure that God remains the strength of your heart. He should remain yours forever.

Hold Onto God!

Help is on the way. I know that you are going through some trials, tribulations, circumstances, and issues. There are storms and all kinds of drama, but the Bible declares that although my health fails and my spirit grows weak, God remains the strength of my heart and he is mine forever.

Hold Onto God!

Even if you don't have enough money, even if you don't have what you might like to have, you should hold onto God no matter what! Even if you feel down and weary, God should remain the strength of your heart. Don't let go of God.

Hold Onto God!

Listen, I didn't say hold onto your friends, to your social media status, to the status quo. Hold onto God, no matter what! I know it's rough, tough, and frustrating, but hold on. Holding onto God means that whatever God's word says, you are holding onto it. If God's word says I'll never leave you; I'm your healer; I'm your strength; I'm your provider; I'm your protector, then hold on.

Hold Onto God!

Your health may fail because of the issues and challenges of life. Your spirit might not feel like doing anything today, but God should be the strength of your heart. They may have given you a pink slip, the doctors may have given you a negative report, but God gets the last word. Your enemies might think they have a plot or a plan, but God has a better plan because he is in control. So, no matter what, hold onto God. Your back may be against the wall but hold onto God.

Hold Onto God!

#justacrumb

Day 24

Give It to Jesus
Mark 9:14-29

Whenever you have a situation or concern about something, it's always a good idea to take it to someone that can handle it. If you need a haircut, you go to a barber or a hairstylist. If you need a manicure or pedicure, you go to a nail technician. If you need legal assistance, you go to a lawyer. If you have health challenges, you go to a doctor. If your children need assistance with their academics, you take the children to a tutor. You go to an individual who is qualified to handle your life's situations. They have the skill and the where-withal and they understand how to deal with anything you might bring to them.

Many of us are taking our situations to the wrong people. Sometimes, we take it to people whom we thought could help us, but find that they have no power either. We even take our dreams, ideas, and concepts to the wrong people. The ones we take them to look like they have it together, but they can't handle it. We struggle when we go to the wrong place, and do not understand that we simply need to bring our situations to Jesus. Do you know what headaches you could alleviate if you would just bring everything to Jesus? Stop trying to come up with your ideas or plans as to how you will work things out. Bring it to Jesus!

In Mark chapter 9, there is a story of a man whose son is possessed. Jesus gets on the scene and sees that people are arguing. Jesus asked what they were arguing about, and the man stands up and explains the situation of his son who is having issues, who is foaming at the mouth and such. The man says to Jesus, "I took him to your disciples because they hang with you, but they couldn't handle it." Jesus turned around and said, "You faithless people." The boy was not delivered because the people around him did not have any faith. Jesus then said, "Bring me the boy." Jesus asked the man how long the boy had been struggling with that condition, and the man explained that it had been happening since the child was a little boy.

You may have been having issues for some years and may have wanted to do some things for some years, but you haven't brought it to Jesus. You doubt that he can handle it. What's crazy is that the man in Mark chapter 9 asks Jesus to help them "if [he] can…" Jesus responded to the man, "What do you mean if I can?" He then explained that anything is possible if a person believes. The man then told Jesus that he believed but that he needed help with his unbelief. This is why you can't take things to just anybody because if they have no faith, their faithlessness might rub off.

When the man brought the child to Jesus, Jesus commanded the spirit to come out of the child and never enter him again. When you bring your situation to Jesus, whatever the problem is, you will never again have to deal with the same issue. You might be facing serious marital problems, health challenges, or financial challenges. But, I just want to encourage you to stop doing it on your own. Stop talking to everyone else, and let him tell you what you're supposed to do.

Give It To Jesus!!

#justacrumb

Day 25

LIVE

W e ought to live soberly. The scriptures tell us that we should not be drunk with wine, but that we should be sober. We should live in such a way that we are thinking clearly, and that is reflective of our relationship and connection with the Lord. The Lord wants full control of your mind. He says not to be drunk with wine because it will ruin your life, but let the Holy Spirit fill you. So, you should live soberly and filled with the Holy Spirit which can lead, guide, and direct you in everything.

You can identify if you are filled with the Holy Spirit just in the way that you speak to others. There should also be songs, and hymns that identify whether you're filled. You should be singing songs of worship and praise. You should communicate with others and greet them with kindness and love.

You need to live in a way that gives thanks to God our father every day for everything. You should give thanks for the good, the bad, the ugly, and even the confusing things. You have to be able to say, "God I don't understand what's going on, but I thank you in the midst of it." When you give God thanks for everything and everything that's going on around you, your mind is not focused on your issues, your drama, or your concerns. There is no need for you to worry about yourself.

Psalm 34:19 tells us, "The righteous person faces many troubles, but the Lord comes to the rescue each time." In other words, through all of your problems, God will deliver you. If God is going to deliver you, what do you think you should do? You should give him thanks for the problems and the issues because he has everything under control. Since he has everything under control, you should do whatever God tells you to do.

Sometimes, you may hit a wall because you are not doing what God told you to do. God gives instructions when you give him thanks when you worship him. He also gives peace. He is going to tell you what you should be doing. You know that God has been speaking something to you. You have to allow him to lead, direct, and guide you. Romans 14:13 tells us, "So let's stop condemning each other. Decide instead to live in such a way that you will not cause another believer to stumble and fall." That means we have to live soberly so that you can hear what God is telling you to do. There are some things you have to stop doing, to correct, to get straight. You have to change some things and live.

Live soberly, live filled, live-giving thanks! Give God thanks for everything: your job, the roof over your head, your car, Uber, even public transportation. You should thank God now because when your breakthrough comes, he won't have to wonder if you are going to show him gratitude. He will remember how you gave him thanks when you were at rock bottom when you were in the midst of your issue when you were in pain. 1 Thessalonians 5:16 tells us, "Rejoice always."

Live! Live clear in your thoughts, clear in your speech, and doing what God is telling you to do. God is saying you're not living because you are not doing what I told you to do.

#justacrumb

BILLY T. STATON, JR.

Made in the USA
Middletown, DE
14 September 2022